# The INSIDE GUIDE

## FAMOUS NATIVE AMERICANS

# Sequoyah

By John Micklos Jr.

Cavendish Square

New York

Published in 2021 by Cavendish Square Publishing, LLC
243 5th Avenue, Suite 136, New York, NY 10016

Copyright © 2021 by Cavendish Square Publishing, LLC

First Edition

Website: cavendishsq.com

Library of Congress Cataloging-in-Publication Data

Names: Micklos, John, author.
Title: Sequoyah / John Micklos, Jr..
Description: First edition. | New York : Cavendish Square Publishing, 2021.
| Series: The Inside Guide: Famous Native Americans | Includes index.
Identifiers: LCCN 2019049420 (print) | LCCN 2019049421 (ebook) | ISBN 9781502651303 (library binding) | ISBN 9781502651280 (paperback) | ISBN 9781502651297 (set) | ISBN 9781502651310 (ebook)
Subjects: LCSH: Sequoyah, 1770?-1843–Juvenile literature. | Cherokee Indians–Biography–Juvenile literature. | Cherokee language–Writing–Juvenile literature. | Cherokee language–Alphabet–Juvenile literature.
Classification: LCC E99.C5 S3849 2021 (print) | LCC E99.C5 (ebook) | DDC 973.04/975570092 [B]–dc23
LC record available at https://lccn.loc.gov/2019049420
LC ebook record available at https://lccn.loc.gov/2019049421

Editor: Kristen Susienka
Copy Editor: Rebecca Rohan
Designer: Deanna Paternostro

CPSIA compliance information: Batch #CS20CSQ: For further information contact Cavendish Square Publishing LLC, New York, New York, at 1-877-980-4450.

Printed in the United States of America

Find us on

# CONTENTS

Chapter One:                                          5
   Native American Histories

Chapter Two:                                         11
   Creating a Written Language

Chapter Three:                                       17
   Changing Times

Chapter Four:                                        23
   A Hero Then and Now

Think About It!                                      28

Timeline                                             29

Glossary                                             30

Find Out More                                        31

Index                                                32

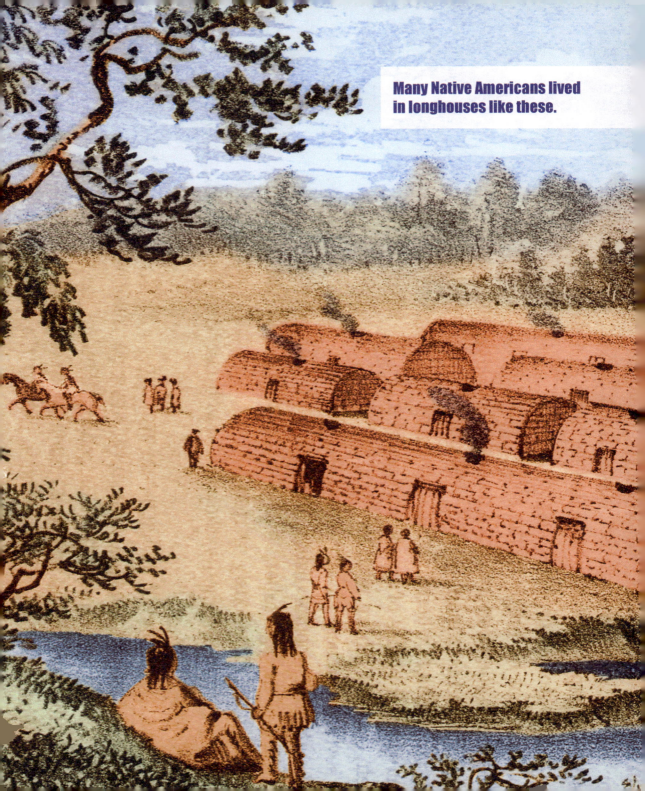

Many Native Americans lived in longhouses like these.

# NATIVE AMERICAN HISTORIES

## Chapter One

**B**efore European settlers arrived in America in the 1500s and 1600s, Native American communities dotted the landscape. Villages and towns were scattered along the coast and far into the interior of the country. Native American communities were often called tribes. They had leaders, warriors, teachers, and healers. Families lived together in homes built from the wood and grass that grew around them. Wars broke out between tribes at times, but other times, people made peace and worked together. In many ways, they weren't too unlike communities today.

## Telling Stories

Native American life often involved storytelling. Almost everything people knew about their beliefs and way of life came from stories. People told them around a fire, on a trail in the woods, or to their families over dinner. Their stories weren't written down. People had to remember them and tell them to others. This was called oral tradition.

## Changing Times

With the arrival of Europeans, life for Native Americans changed. Over a few decades, the land they'd lived on for generations became

Life changed for the Native Americans once Europeans began building settlements.

overrun by settlers, who built their own villages and communities. Forests were cut down, and many native people struggled to keep their traditions, languages, and **cultures** alive. Many European settlers wanted the native people to live, speak, and act just like them.

Native Americans are shown here watching English settlers.

# Sequoyah

In the 1800s, a Native American man named Sequoyah brought another change to his native Cherokee community. This change centered on how Cherokee stories and traditions were shared. Sequoyah developed a writing tool called a **syllabary**.

Sequoyah invented a writing system for the Cherokee language.

**Fast Fact**
Sequoyah never learned to read, write, or speak English.

# THE AGE OF DISCOVERY

The Age of Discovery happened between the 15th and 17th centuries. European ships sailed the waters looking for new trading routes and places to start colonies. This was a time when Spain, France, Britain, and other nations tried to become the most dominant country in other parts of the world. By the time Sequoyah was born in the later 1700s, this era had ended. However, the world Sequoyah entered was one in which Britain had become a powerful force in North America because of the Age of Discovery.

The first Europeans arrived in North America on tall ships like these.

This syllabary created the first written language of a Native American tribe. It was later used by many men and women to write down the legends and history of the Cherokee.

Sequoyah allowed the Cheokee's stories to be **preserved**, but he also changed the main way stories were told and the Cherokee language was learned. Today, oral tradition is still a way of passing down history and information about a tribe to others in the community, but writing is also used. Without Sequoyah, some native tales might have been forgotten. He helped a community tell its story to others and to future generations. Because of Sequoyah, the Cherokee had their own written language and the power that comes with it.

**Fast Fact**

Sequoyah's daughter helped him popularize the written Cherokee language.

Here, Sequoyah holds a copy of the syllabary he created.

# CREATING A WRITTEN LANGUAGE

**R**eading and writing are parts of daily life for many people in the world. Most people know how to use letters in the alphabet to spell their names and other words. They can write stories with those words and use words to describe their families, their hobbies, or their favorite things.

Creating a new writing system isn't easy. It takes time, patience, and teamwork. However, Sequoyah proved it can be done when he alone created a written language for the Cherokee.

## About Sequoyah

No one knows when Sequoyah was born. The Cherokee people didn't keep records of such things. We know he was born in what's now eastern Tennessee. Historians believe he was born between 1765 and 1775.

Sequoyah's mother was a Cherokee. Her name was Wuh-teh. His father was most likely a white man named Nathaniel Gist. Gist came from Virginia. He worked as a fur trader and traded with the Native Americans in the area. He also fought in the French and Indian War and the American Revolution. Sequoyah was raised by his mother. He didn't know his father. Later in life, Sequoyah said his English name was George Guest or Guess. Some people think these are different ways of saying the name Gist. However, other people don't believe Gist was his father.

George Washington led troops in both the French and Indian War and the American Revolution before becoming president.

People who met Sequoyah noticed he walked with a limp. He was said to have been born with it. As an adult, Sequoyah worked as a silversmith and blacksmith. That meant he could make beautiful objects out of silver and iron. Blacksmiths also repaired damaged objects and made other tools for work or for war. One of Sequoyah's favorite things to do, though, was paint.

## "Talking Leaves"

As a young man, Sequoyah had seen white families in the area where he lived. The United States was its own country

Many Cherokee people lived in houses made of woven sticks covered in mud. In the summer, they lived in open-air houses.

by that time, and the newly independent American families built villages and towns near Native American lands.

Sequoyah watched the settlers share written messages. He called the written papers "talking leaves." At the time, the Cherokee had no writing system. They shared everything through speaking. Some Cherokee believed writing was magic. Sequoyah knew better. He knew writing was simply a way of sharing ideas. He believed the written messages gave white people power. He wanted that kind of power for the Cherokee too.

Sequoyah believed that if the Cherokee had a written language, they could also record their culture. Then, their children and grandchildren could read what had been written and learn about their history.

In 1809, Sequoyah began working to create a writing system for the Cherokee language. Some friends thought he was silly. Others thought he was taking part in **witchcraft**.

## Fast Fact

In 1825, Sequoyah's language became the official written language of the Cherokee Nation.

Creating a writing system was hard! First, Sequoyah tried using a symbol for each sentence. That was too hard. Next, he tried using a symbol for each word. There were too many words. That meant too many symbols. Then, he matched symbols to each syllable, or word section, in the language. He spent years

# SEQUOYAH AND THE BATTLE OF HORSESHOE BEND

Sequoyah was a soldier during the War of 1812, which lasted from 1812 to 1814 and was between the United States and Britain. However, many Native American tribes fought too. One group was the Creek. There were two divisions of Creek, Upper and Lower. Members of the Lower Creek supported the United States and wanted to become a **sovereign** group like the Cherokee. The Upper Creek wanted to keep its lifestyle and traditions. This disagreement led to the Battle of Horseshoe Bend in 1814. Sequoyah joined the US Army. He was one of almost 500 Cherokee who joined that side. Some Cherokee followed American rules and laws. For that reason, they were called a "civilized tribe." They agreed to help the United States. In the end, hundreds of Creek men, women, and children were killed. The US government also gained over 20 million acres (8 million hectares) of Creek land.

This is a scene from the Battle of Horseshoe Bend.

creating this system, called a syllabary. When finished, it contained more than 80 symbols. The English alphabet has just 26 letters.

In 1815, Sequoyah married a Cherokee woman named Sally Waters. They had a daughter named Ayoka. Ayoka became the first Cherokee to learn to read and write using Sequoyah's system.

## Getting Others to Believe

At first, the other Cherokee didn't believe in Sequoyah's system. With the help of Ayoka, he convinced them it worked. Over time, nearly all Cherokee learned to read and write. Sequoyah became a hero. Although he died in 1843, he knew his writing system would live on. Today, the Cherokee still remember Sequoyah. The written language he invented is still used and taught.

**Sequoyah's syllabary included all of the syllables in the Cherokee language.**

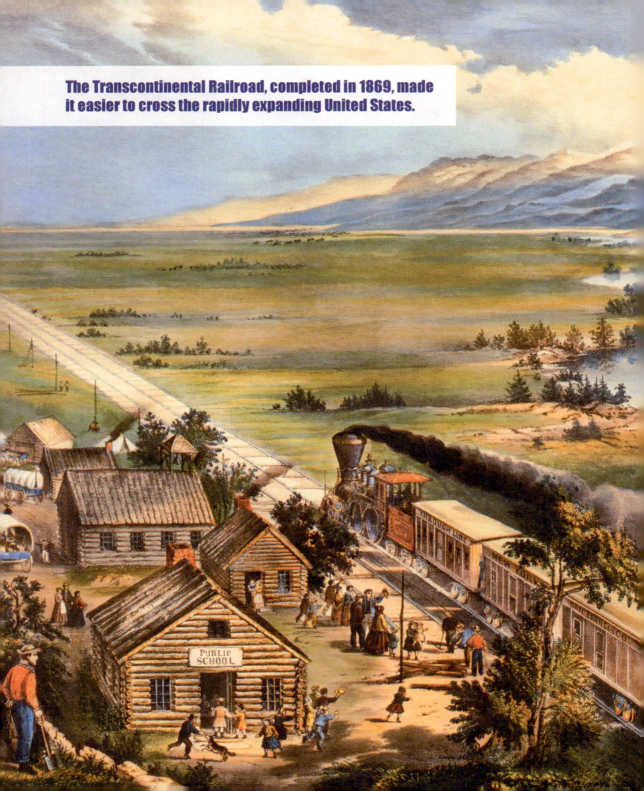
The Transcontinental Railroad, completed in 1869, made it easier to cross the rapidly expanding United States.

# CHANGING TIMES

## Chapter Three

The Cherokee had known of the white man for hundreds of years. The first European explorer to meet a Cherokee tribe was Hernando de Soto in the 1500s. By the time Sequoyah was born in the late 1700s, white settlers had made America their home alongside Native Americans. However, struggles between white people and native people created difficulties for both sides.

## Settling

At the beginning of European settlement, there were only a few settlers to worry about. Some Native Americans tried fights or **raids** to stop the settlers, but settlements continued to be built. More settlers soon arrived. They brought with them new tools, new ways of thinking and talking, and new beliefs.

Many white settlers thought the native people were **inferior**. They didn't believe the Native American way of life was good. White settlers also believed the United States should grow and become a more powerful nation. The only way to grow was to move into places where Native Americans lived. Once there, the white people tried to force many natives to live as they did.

**Fast Fact**

Within 10 years after Sequoyah introduced his writing system, nearly all Cherokee could read and write.

**The Cherokee hunted deer, rabbits, and other animals for food.**

Over time, the settlers changed the Cherokee way of life. The Cherokee could no longer travel wherever they wanted. Their hunting lands became towns or villages that looked like European cities. Good farming land was taken over too. This meant the Cherokee couldn't grow as many crops.

Settlers also hunted animals that were important to the Cherokee, like deer. Fighting broke out between the Cherokee and the settlers. Battles took place off and on for decades. In the 1830s, the US government stepped in, leading to difficult times for Native American groups, especially the Cherokee.

## Losing Their Land

During Sequoyah's life, the US government and the Cherokee signed **treaties**. Sequoyah himself was even involved in some of these treaties. These agreements took away land from the native people and gave

**The *Cherokee Phoenix* newspaper is shown here.**

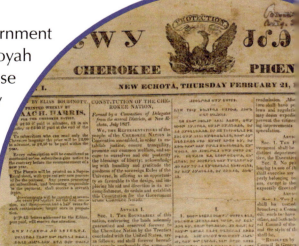

**Cherokee chief John Ross tried to resist the efforts to take Cherokee land.**

it to settlers. Soon, the Cherokee had very little land left. In the Treaty of New Echota of 1835, Cherokee chiefs agreed to move their people to **reservations** in a part of the country called Indian Territory. However, not everyone moved.

In 1838, roughly 15,000 Cherokee still remained in the East. They were forced to leave. The US government could do this because of the **Indian Removal Act** of 1830. The Cherokee had to travel more than 1,000 miles (1,600 kilometers) to Indian Territory, in what's now Oklahoma. The trip took many months. About 4,000 Cherokee died along the way. The deadly trip became known as the Trail of Tears.

## Old Settlers

Before the Trail of Tears, some Cherokee adopted the ways of the white settlers. Others moved west of the Mississippi River. They set up a government there. They lived peacefully, far away from the white settlers. Sequoyah moved west in the 1820s. He took his family with him. Those who left early were called "Old Settlers."

### Fast Fact

The *Cherokee Phoenix* was the first national **bilingual** newspaper in the United States. It was published in Cherokee and English.

19

# A LIFE IN OKLAHOMA

Once at the reservation in Oklahoma, the Cherokee Nation rebuilt. They passed a new constitution in 1839 and built their own Supreme Court building in 1844. Many Cherokee wanted the tribe to be its own country, like the United States was. Today, it's a sovereign government within the United States. It has its own leaders, its own government, its own police force, its own schools, and its own courts. It's a nation within a nation. This allows the Cherokee traditions to continue and their language to thrive.

The Cherokee remain among the best-known Native American tribes. Many Cherokee live on land set aside for them in Oklahoma and North Carolina. The Cherokee Nation has more than 300,000 members. That's the most of any Native American tribe in the United States.

Today, most Cherokee people live on Cherokee lands in Oklahoma and North Carolina.

## Cherokee Language

After it was completed in 1821, Sequoyah's writing system spread among the Cherokee. It continued spreading even when white people took more Cherokee land. In 1825, the

Cherokee made Sequoyah's syllabary their official written language. That year, the Cherokee Nation also bought a printing press. They published a constitution, written in the Cherokee language. They even created a newspaper called the *Cherokee Phoenix* written in Cherokee. It brought them together. It made them similar to but different from the white settlers.

Approximately 4,000 Cherokee died on the journey west after they were forced from their lands. The journey became known as the Trail of Tears.

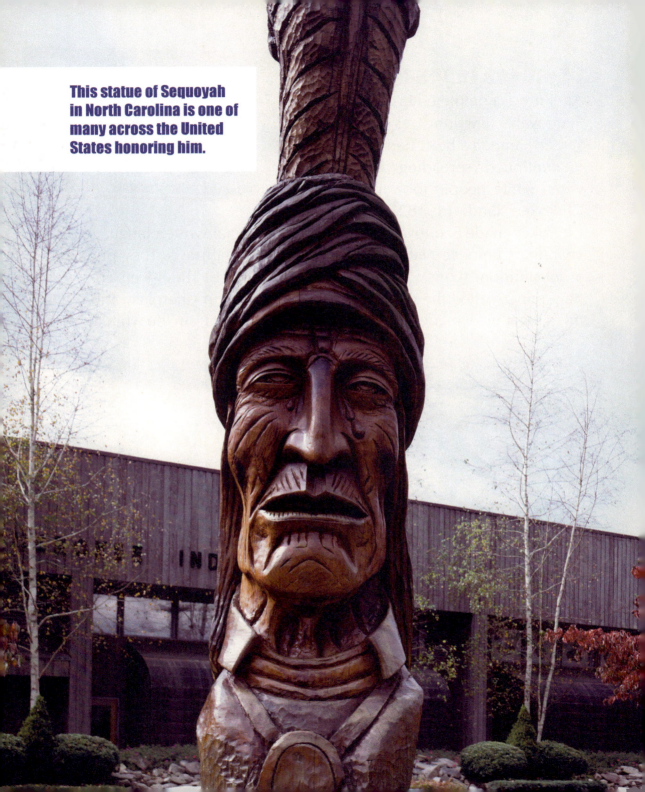

This statue of Sequoyah in North Carolina is one of many across the United States honoring him.

# A HERO THEN AND NOW

## Chapter Four

Sequoyah didn't start out as a hero to his people, but he became one. At first, other Cherokee didn't believe in his writing system. Some made fun of him. Others thought he was creating witchcraft instead of a language. His own wife thought he was wasting his time and doing something impossible. In fact, it's said that she burned many of his papers. Over time, though, she began to understand and support his work.

Other people knew just how special his creation was. His daughter Ayoka helped him test the written language and prove it could be learned. Politician Sam Houston also believed. He was a friend of the Cherokee. They made him an adopted member of the Cherokee Nation. Houston said, "Your invention of the alphabet is worth more to your people than two bags full of gold in the hands of every Cherokee."

## A Language That Lasts

Today, Sequoyah is truly a hero to his tribe and to others around the world. He helped the Cherokee

### Fast Fact

The Eastern Band of Cherokee run the Kituwah Preservation and Education Program and also have a school dedicated to preserving the Cherokee language. It's called the New Kituwah Academy.

**By creating a written language, Sequoyah allowed the Cherokee people to pass on their history and culture to future generations.**

tribe keep its traditions alive, even when they were pressured to lose them to the white man's culture. The written language he created gave the Cherokee people the chance to learn to read and write in the language of their community.

Most writing systems were developed over many years. Many people helped create them. Sequoyah developed the Cherokee writing system alone. It took him 12 years. He's one of the most influential inventors in Native American history.

Over time, many Native American languages have faded away. Some have totally disappeared. Even the Cherokee language is used less than it was in the past. Today, most Cherokee speak English. Only about 20,000 people speak Cherokee. However, many people remain interested in the

Cherokee language. Several universities offer courses on reading and writing Cherokee. Sequoyah's system is simple to learn, so it remains a living language.

## Accepting Sequoyah

The Cherokee Nation knew how important Sequoyah's writing system was to their culture. A few years after it was introduced, they wanted to honor him. In 1825, they gave him a silver medal showing his face. It was to thank him for his gift to the Cherokee people.

Would Sequoyah be surprised that people still use his writing system after 200 years? Probably not. He knew the power of the written word. Because of him, the Cherokee have a written history of their culture. Thousands of documents have been printed in the Cherokee language. This means the tribe's history will live on forever.

Many people are still amazed that a single person created this writing system. Sequoyah's work draws praise from many people. "He brought our people literacy and the gift of communicating through long distances and the ages," says the Cherokee Nation website. "This one person brought to his people this great gift without hired educators, no books, and no cost." Without him, the Cherokee might not have a written language of their own to read or write.

## Remembering Sequoyah

Sequoyah is remembered in a number of ways today. First, he's remembered through the written language he created. Second, he's remembered through statues, books, and museums. Many things and places have also been named in his honor.

# SHARING THE LANGUAGE

Today, efforts are being made to keep the Cherokee language alive. Several language preservation groups have appeared since 2005, when the number of **fluent** speakers dropped to 460. One group is the Cherokee Preservation Foundation. It works to raise money that's used to buy teaching materials, start and support language-learning classes within the wider community, create a degree for teachers wanting to teach Cherokee, host events that allow fluent Cherokee speakers to talk with others in the language, and support scholarships that help other learners become experts in Cherokee. It works closely with other Cherokee groups to help make the language available to others. An example is the Kituwah Preservation and Education Program, which received one of the Cherokee Preservation Foundation's first investments. It has worked hard to create more Cherokee speakers and expose others in the wider community to the Cherokee language.

**Shown here is Sequoyah's official stamp.**

USA
19c
Sequoyah

The Sequoyah Birthplace Museum in eastern Tennessee stands near the place where it's thought Sequoyah was born. It takes visitors on a walk through his life and work. Every August, it honors Sequoyah Remembrance Day with tribal events, blacksmith demonstrations, basket making, educational talks, and costumed characters.

Other ways Sequoyah has been honored include a movie called *Sequoyah: The Great Teacher of*

**Fast Fact**
A stamp with Sequoyah's image on it was released in 1980.

*the Cherokee Nation* that was made in 1974. In addition, the state of Oklahoma's Library Association gives a Sequoyah Book Award each year. In 1917, a statue of Sequoyah was **installed** at the US Capitol Building. He's one of 100 famous people to have a statue in the building's National Statuary Hall. Finally, the giant sequoia tree is said to have been named after him.

It's clear Sequoyah will continue to be remembered throughout history for his achievements. He not only affected the lives of his people but also served as a **role model** for others with his dedication to the written word and to keeping his culture alive long after he was gone.

**Many people believe that the sequoia trees of California are named after Sequoyah.**

**Use these questions to help you think more deeply about this topic.**

1. Imagine what it would be like if you could only talk and not write. How would life be different for you? How would you tell stories? How would you share information about yourself?

2. How were the first Native American communities similar to US communities today?

3. Imagine you had to come up with a new language. What things would be important to consider when creating it?

4. Who helped Sequoyah test his new language?

5. In what ways did Sequoyah help his people with his syllabary?

# TIMELINE

| Sequoyah's Life | World Events |
|---|---|

**1765–1775**
Sequoyah is born sometime during these years.

**1776**
The United States of America is formed.

**1809**
Sequoyah begins work on his syllabary.

**1812**
The United States and Great Britain go to war. The War of 1812 draws in many Native American tribes, including the Cherokee.

**1814**
Sequoyah fights in the Battle of Horseshoe Bend.

**1821**
Sequoyah finishes his syllabary.

**1830**
The Indian Removal Act is signed.

**1838–1839**
Thousands of Cherokee die as they are forced to move west on the Trail of Tears.

**1843**
Sequoyah dies, but he knows his writing system will live on.

# GLOSSARY

**bilingual:** Relating to the use of two languages.

**culture:** The beliefs and ways of life of a certain group of people.

**federally recognized:** Given official acknowledgement and money by the national government.

**fluent:** Able to speak and understand a language perfectly.

**Indian Removal Act:** A law in 1830 that let the US government move Native Americans living in the South to reservations in the West.

**inferior:** Beneath; less than.

**install:** To put in place.

**preserve:** To keep safe or protect.

**raid:** A surprise attack on a village or group.

**reservation:** Land set aside for Native American tribes to live on.

**role model:** Someone who others look up to as an example of a good person or leader.

**sovereign:** Independent or able to make decisions without approval from another group.

**syllabary:** A set of written symbols that stand for syllables.

**treaty:** A written agreement between two groups that ends fights or problems between them.

**witchcraft:** Magic or powerful spells.

# FIND OUT MORE

## Books

Rogers, Kelly. *Sequoyah and the Written Word*. Huntington Beach, CA: Teacher Created Materials, 2016.

Rumford, James. *Sequoyah: The Cherokee Man Who Gave His People Writing*. Translated by Anna Sixkiller Huckaby. New York, NY: Houghton Mifflin, 2004.

## Websites

### Cherokee Preservation Foundation
*cherokeepreservation.org*
This website provides information about the Cherokee Preservation Foundation and its goals, as well as what it has accomplished since its beginnings.

### Sequoyah Birthplace Museum
*www.sequoyahmuseum.org*
This website has many facts and stories about Sequoyah and his work.

### "Talking Leaves"
*videos.oeta.tv/video/talking-leaves-ainjmk*
This video gives a good overview of Sequoyah's life and how he developed the syllabary.

# INDEX

**A**
Ayoka, 15, 23

**B**
Battle of Horseshoe
    Bend, 14–15
bilingual, 19
blacksmith, 12, 26

**C**
Cherokee Nation, 13,
    20–21, 23, 25, 27
*Cherokee Phoenix*,
    the, 18-19, 21
culture, 6, 13, 24–25,
    27

**F**
federally recognized,
    21
fluent, 26

**I**
Indian Removal Act,
    19
inferior, 17
install, 27

**J**
Jamestown, Virginia, 6

**K**
Kituwah Preservation
    and Education
    Program, 23, 26

**O**
oral tradition, 5, 9

**P**
preserve, 9, 23, 26

**R**
raid, 17
reservation, 19–20
role model, 27

**S**
settlers, 5–6, 13,
    17–19, 21
sovereign, 14, 20
syllabary, 7, 10, 15,
    21

**T**
"talking leaves,"
    12–13
Trail of Tears, 19, 21
treaties, 18–19

**W**
War of 1812, 14
witchcraft, 13, 23